Günter Schneider (Photos) and Clemens Beeck

FASCINATING DRESDEN

Stunning Pictures of "Florence on the Elbe"

Jaron Verlag

The Fascinating City on the Elbe

With its monuments of sandstone and its location on the picturesque Elbe River, Dresden's unmistakable cityscape elicits words of admiration from every viewer. A combination of fascination and awe accompany visitors as they wander through the Zwinger, enter the Semperoper (Semper Opera House), visit the Grünes Gewölbe (Green Vault) in the Royal Palace or stroll along the Bruehl Terrace. The abundance of beautiful sights one encounters in Dresden is virtually overwhelming.

Dresden is characterized by an exuberance of the Baroque, which was able to develop here in all its glory. The magnificent Augustan era began in 1694 when Friedrich August I, often referred to as August the Strong, became Elector of Saxony. The ruler brought together the best masters of their trades and transformed the royal seat into a Baroque city of European stature. His son Friedrich August II continued these efforts when, in 1733, he called luminaries of the Habsburg monarchy to the city on the Elbe. The artistry of the two rulers laid the foundation for the cultural city of Dresden, which continues to enjoy an international reputation thanks to its outstanding art collections. As the "German Florence," Gottfried Herder praised Dresden and its unique art treasures.

The nickname "Florence on the Elbe" is no accident. As early as the Renaissance, Italian artists and builders were active in Dresden. Their valuable knowledge and masterful skills were to benefit the city after the Albertine line of Wettin rulers, who had made Dresden their official residence and seat in 1485, became the electors of Saxony in 1547. The impressive Royal Palace attests to this first cultural awakening.

Time and again, Dresden has attracted outstanding representatives of the arts, figures such as Friedrich Schiller, Richard Wagner, Gottfried Semper and Oskar Kokoschka, and all these artists left their mark on Dresden. Composer Carl Maria von Weber revolutionized German opera. The painters Caspar David Friedrich and Adrian Ludwig Richter made the Saxon capital c a hotbed of romance; Ernst Ludwig Kirchner and H fellow artists of the "Brücke" movement influenced G man Expressionism. Born in Dresden, the world famo painter Gerhard Richter is one of the most importa representatives of contemporary art.

In its more than 800-year history, the city on the Elb has also suffered painful periods. The Seven Years' W brought a violent end to the Augustan era in 1760. Th destruction of the city's center three months before th end of World War II was its historical low point: Th heavy air raids of February 1945 transformed the c tural metropolis into a field of rubble.

After decades of living with these ruins as reminde of the horrors of war, Dresden – the capital of the Fre State of Saxony – began an amazing Renaissance 1990. The reconstruction of the Baroque Frauenkirch from 1993 to 2004 completed not only the belove urban silhouette, but signaled the return of Baroqu splendor to the city's historic center. Dresden regaine its civic identity, one building at a time. Faithfully r constructed Baroque and Rococo townhouses arour the New Market Square steadily attracted a growir number of visitors.

The Royal Palace's magnificent Renaissance sgraffi facades once again shine in all their glory. In its r stored rooms, particularly in the Grünes Gewölbe, th spectacular art treasures of the Wettin rulers sparkl With the Gothic Palace Chapel, Dresden has regaine an iconic venue of its centuries-old musical tradition. E by bit, the city's unique museum landscape has bee enriched with new attractions.

This illustrated book presents – in beautiful images not only the main attractions located in Dresder historic Old Town, but also takes the reader into th city's New Town and to Loschwitz, home of the Pillni and Moritzburg Castles. The book leads readers c a journey through one of the most beautiful cities Europe.

P.Z. - DRESDEN - ALTMARKT

Until the mid-19th century, the Baroque style set the tone in **Old Dresden**. The Catholic Court Church, situated at the end of the famous Augustus Bridge, dominated the Elbe panorama of the residential city of the Kingdom of Saxony (top right). The Royal Palace, located behind the church, is barely visible in the photograph. Next to the church, one can clearly see Gottfried Semper's Royal Court Theatre, which building burned to the ground in 1869, just a few years after this historic photograph was taken. It was later replaced by the Semper Opera.

In 1900, Dresden was a burgeoning metropolis with half a million inhabitants. Yet, the center of this city on the Elbe had maintained its relaxed character. Old Market Square was surrounded by town houses from the Baroque and Renaissance periods (left). Unveile in 1880, the victory monument, with a statue of Germania, stoo in the center of the square. The Kreuzkirche is visible in the bac ground.

In the 1930s, automobiles and other motorized vehicles st drove on New Market Square (bottom right). The hotel Stac Berlin, which is located next to the Frauenkirche, was famous fo its beauty.

Inspired by the unique appeal of his birthplace, in 1957 th author Erich Kästner wrote in a memoir about his childhood: "Th fact (...) that I recognize not only the bad and ugly, but also th beautiful, is a gift I owe to having grown up in Dresden."

Those visiting Dresden today will find it hard to imagine that this magnificent city lay in ruins just 70 years ago (below: View of the historic New Town; top right: Prager Strasse).

Until early 1945, Dresden had largely been spared by World War II. All the more terrible was the work of destruction caused by the British and American air raids that took place from 13 to 15 February 1945. In four waves of attack within 38 hours, the cultural metropolis was razed to the ground. "Anyone who has forgotten how to cry will learn this again during the **Destruction of Dresden**" noted the deeply shaken writer Gerhart Haupt-mann (1862–1946), who watched the inferno from Loschwitz Hill.

The bombing caused a murderous firestorm with temperatures more than 800 degrees from which very few residents living on the banks of the Elbe could escape. At least 25,000 people died according to official estimates (top left), including refugees, prisoners of war and forced laborers of the Nazi dictatorship.

Today Dresden has literally risen from the ashes, but the consequences of the air strike shortly before the war's end are still visible in the cityscape.

hose who look across the river Elbe from the bank of the New own towards Old Dresden cannot help but feel enchanted. The icturesque backdrop of Baroque architecture, natural meadows nd flowing water looks like a beautifully arranged painting. The armonious interplay between the flowing current and the city's anorama is of unique beauty, unparalleled in the world. The alian painter Bernardo Bellotto (1721–80), known as Canalet- o, captured views of the Augustus Bridge, Bruehl's Terrace, the rauenkirche and Hofkirche for all eternity. A red easel on the hore near the Augustus Bridge shows the spot where, in 1748, he most famous painting of Dresden was created: the "Canaletto /iew" (bottom left). The painting's real name is "Dresden from the Right Bank of the Elbe with the Augustus Bridge" (above) and is on view in the Gemäldegalerie.

The nearly four-hundred-meter-long **Augustus Bridge** is one of the most historic river crossings in Europe. Constructed in the 13th century as one of the earliest stone bridges in Central Europe, it connects the historic parts of the Old Town and the modern New Town (bottom right). August the Strong had the bridge reconstruct- ed from 1727 to 1731 by Matthäus Daniel Pöppelmann and Johann Gottfried Fehre. In 1910 it had to be reconstructed.

The sculpture "Surge," situated on the main pillar of the bridge, recalls the "flood of the century", which took place in 2002 (bottom middle).

9

Grouped around **Theater Square** are Baroque and Renaissance sandstone buildings of distinction: the Royal Palace, the Catholic Court Church, the Gemäldegalerie (Painting Gallery) and the Semperoper. As stone symbols of the crown, clergy and culture, they constitute a Saxon state forum. Gottfried Semper, architect of the opera house, wished to create a stately square on the Elbe. The name of the square alludes to the fact that, since the 17th century, seven different theaters have been located on this site.

Smaller buildings complete the splendid impression of the square. The Old Town's guardhouse on the southern edge, built 1830–32, was designed by the Prussian architect Karl Friedrich Schinkel (bottom right). Modeled after a temple, the Classical structure something one would expect to find in Berlin rather than in Dresden; it served as a central theater box office.

The Italian Village, an inn built in 1913, borders the squa towards the Elbe. The establishment's curious name with th magnificent ceiling paintings (top right) is reminiscent of dwellin quarters of the Italian builders and artisans who constructed th Baroque Court Church in the 18th century (top left).

The work of sculptor Johannes Schilling, an equestrian statue the center of Theater Square, represents King Johann, who rule Saxony from 1854 to 1873 (bottom left). It was unveiled in 1889

Dresden owes its worldwide reputation as a cultural city of statur
to a great many things, not least to the **Semperoper**. Locate
on Theatre Square, the venue of the Saxon State Opera an
Staatskapelle Dresden is an icon of the music world. This gem c
European stage architecture is the second theater Gottfried Ser
per (1803–79) realized at this location. His first design, the Royc
Court Theatre, opened its doors in 1841. But the building in whic
Richard Wagner's operas "Rienzi," "The Flying Dutchman" an
"Tannhäuser" celebrated their premiers was destroyed in a fir
nearly three decades later.

In its place, between 1871 and 1878, one of the most prestigiou
opera houses in Europe was built in the style of the Italian Hig
Renaissance according to Semper's plans. Unmistakable is its im
posing portal with the Panther Quadriga (previous double page)
On either side of the entrance is a sculpture created by Ernst Rie
schel: the seated figures of Goethe (below) and Schiller.

After its destruction in World War II, the Semperoper was faithfull
reconstructed beginning in 1977. Its foyers, staircases and audito
rium (above) are just as magnificent and noble as they once were
On February 13, 1985, the reopening of Dresden's landmar
was celebrated with a performance of the opera "Der Freischütz
by Carl Maria von Weber.

ugust the Strong was so obsessed with Constanze von Hoym – ho was ten years his junior – that he had a palace built for his eloved next to his own castle. In 1708, his beautiful mistress, ow appointed Countess of Cosel, moved into the luxuriously fur- shed **Taschenberg Palace** (above). After the prominent couple ad fallen out, the countess was forced to trade her glamourous e in the court for a lackluster existence at Stolpen Castle, to hich she was banished in 1716 and where she remained until er death in 1765.

enceforth, the Wettiner crown prince resided in the mistress's rmer city palace. With the increasing demands of the heir to e throne, the building was enlarged, reaching its present size etween 1756 and 1767. The Rococo halls were among the ost magnificent interiors of Dresden.

nce its reconstruction from 1992 to 1995, the former love nest f August the Strong has been a modern luxury hotel, where prom- ent figures like Barack Obama and Vladimir Putin have spent the ght (below).

ituated between the Taschenberg and Zwinger Palaces, the neo- Gothic Cholera Fountain by Gottfried Semper was built in 1843 ut of gratitude that Dresden had been spared recent cholera epi- emics. Also worth a visit is the Neo-Baroque theater located near ost Square whose curtain rose for the first time in 1913.

Built in 1847–55, the **Gemäldegalerie** (Painting Gallery) is one of the most prestigious museums in Germany; it was the second famous cultural building Gottfried Semper realized on Dresden's Theatre Square (top right). With it, the fine art collection of the Saxon electors and kings was given a worthy architectural framework. Gottfried Semper (1803–79), a Hamburg native, integrated the Italian High Renaissance style building into the still open flank of the Zwinger Palace (bottom left).

The most famous artwork in the Gemäldegalerie Alte Meister (Old Masters Painting Gallery) was already admired by Goethe when it was exhibited in the Johanneum. The "Sistine Madonna" by Italian artist Raphael (top left) came into the possession of the Wettin court in 1754, after it was discovered in and acquired from the San Sisto Convent in Piacenza. This Renaissance masterpiece, with the frequently satirized cherub faces at the bottom, is one of the most famous paintings of all time.

A visit to the Gemäldegalerie is a treat for art lovers not just thanks to its world-famous works of the Italian Renaissance, but also those by great artists such as Anthony van Dyck, Jan van Eyck, Rembrandt, Peter Paul Rubens, Lucas Cranach the Elder, Albrecht Dürer and Hans Holbein.

Renowned works exhibited here in the museum include "The Chocolate Girl," which was painted in 1745 by the Swiss artist Jean-Étienne Liotard (bottom right).

The construction of the **Catholic Court Church** was a highly controversial matter. The fact that Friedrich August II began building a Catholic cathedral in 1739 in the heartland of the Reformation caused quite an uproar. But, because the Saxon ruler was also King of Poland, he was also a member of the Catholic community.

The building contract was awarded to Gaetano Chiaveri of Rome, who created a place of worship in the expressive style of the Late Roman Baroque in a prominent location in the city (left). The 78 religious figures with which sculptor Lorenzo Mattielli embellished the mighty nave particularly enhanced the building's sacred aura (above middle). The Venetian was one of the most sought-after Baroque artists in Europe. The church's altarpiece was executed in Rome between 1752 and 1761 by the Dresden court painter Anton Raphael Mengs (right).

The church was completed in 1755 and is dedicated to the Holy Trinity, its namesake. Its graceful tower dominates the famous silhouette of Dresden's Old Town. Because Catholic services were not well received by the city's citizens, processions took place in an ambulatory inside the church.

The Catholic Wettiners were laid to rest in the crypt (below middle). However, only the heart of August the Strong lies here: his remains are buried in Krakow Cathedral.

The **Zwinger** (previous double page) is an outstanding piece of Baroque architecture, and was created three hundred years ago as the work of an ideally-matched cooperation between the architect Matthäus Daniel Pöppelmann (1662–1736) and the sculptor Balthasar Permoser (1651–1732). It testifies to the courtly splendor of the Augustan age, combining its representative function with a jovial atmosphere.

When work began on Dresden's world-famous structure in 1709, August the Strong only planned to create an orangery and a garden as an atrium for a new palace that was to be constructed along the Elbe. As King of Poland and as a symbol of his claim to power, however, he developed the Zwinger into a magnificent festival ground, framed by ornate pavilions and galleries. The majestic Crown Gate along the Zwinger's moat (above), the opulently decorated Rampart Pavilion (below) – a virtuoso work of Rococo art – and the neighboring Nymphs' Bath fountain, with its sensuous sculptures and rushing cascades, are among the most impressive elements that characterize the Zwinger.

In the mid-19th century, the Baroque artwork was closed toward the Elbe with Semper's Gemäldegalerie, a museum complex in the Renaissance style.

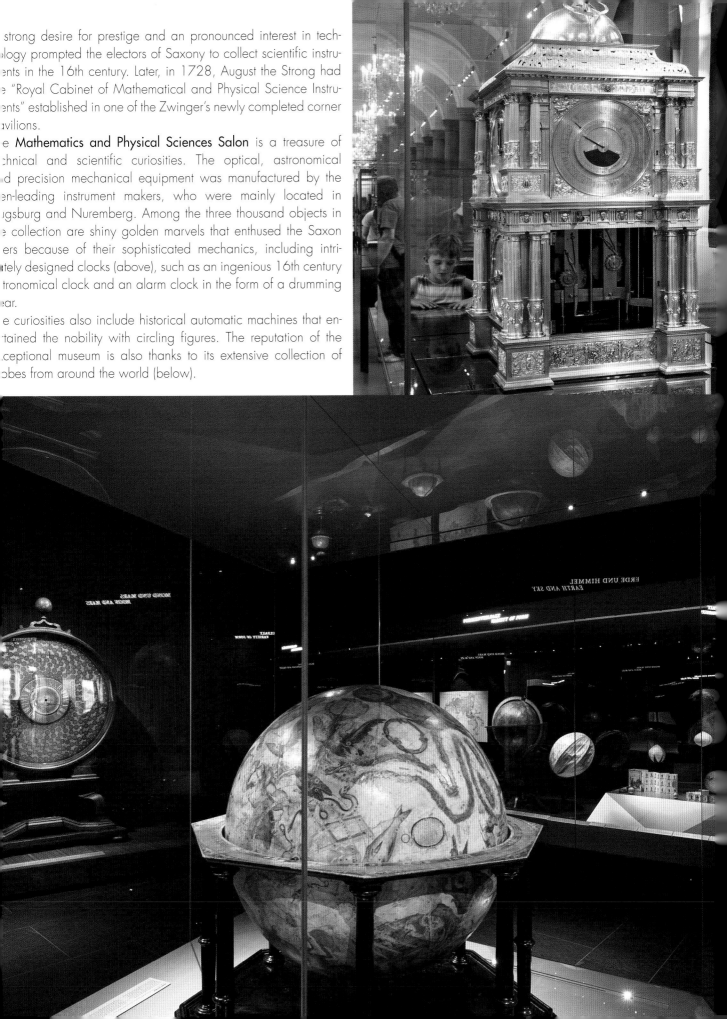

strong desire for prestige and an pronounced interest in tech-
ology prompted the electors of Saxony to collect scientific instru-
ents in the 16th century. Later, in 1728, August the Strong had
e "Royal Cabinet of Mathematical and Physical Science Instru-
ents" established in one of the Zwinger's newly completed corner
avilions.

e **Mathematics and Physical Sciences Salon** is a treasure of
chnical and scientific curiosities. The optical, astronomical
d precision mechanical equipment was manufactured by the
en-leading instrument makers, who were mainly located in
ugsburg and Nuremberg. Among the three thousand objects in
e collection are shiny golden marvels that enthused the Saxon
ers because of their sophisticated mechanics, including intri-
tely designed clocks (above), such as an ingenious 16th century
tronomical clock and an alarm clock in the form of a drumming
ear.

e curiosities also include historical automatic machines that en-
tained the nobility with circling figures. The reputation of the
ceptional museum is also thanks to its extensive collection of
obes from around the world (below).

One of the Zwinger's most admired collections is its **Porcelai**
Collection, created by August the Strong in 1715. The 20,0C
exhibits include works from Saxon's original porcelain culture a
well as traditional Chinese and Japanese porcelain from the f
mous Saxon elector's famous collections.

Saxon alchemist Johann Friedrich Böttger and physicist Walth
von Tschirnhaus succeeded for the first time in Europe in creatir
"white gold" (porcelain) in 1708. This led to August the Strong
founding of the Meissner Manufaktur, which created the majori
of fascinating artworks – from the heydays of the Baroque ar
Rococo periods – found in the collection (above). One modeler
particular, Johann Joachim Kändler (1706–75), crafted grandios
sculptural artworks from this material.

During the Age of Absolutism, porcelain from China and Japc
was a popular status symbol. High "dragoon vases," whic
August the Strong acquired from the Prussian King Friedrich W
helm I in exchange for approximately six hundred horsemen fro
Saxony's army, are in the exhibition. The abundance of porcela
from China and Japan in the Oriental Gallery (below) illustrates th
elector's passion for collecting. The presentation of the 17th an
18th centuries works was then customary in the court.

The building on the Marien Bridge seems to have sprung out of a tale from the One Thousand and One Nights. In reality, the magical backdrop served as a highly visible marketing symbol for the cigarette brand **Yenidze**, whose product was manufactured in the building. The industrialist Hugo Zietz built his tobacco factory within sight of the Zwinger (below). Based on the monumental Caliph's tomb in Cairo, its minaret-like chimney and echoes of Moorish architecture make the former factory look like a mosque.

The iridescent dome (above) shone as a prominent advertisement in the night sky of Dresden, where, at the time, nearly 40 cigarette manufacturers competed with one another. Since then, the building, which Dresdeners initially vehemently rejected, has lent an oriental accent to the city's distinctive skyline. The fairytale-like factory did not prove fortuitous for its architect, Martin Hammitzsch: his creation got him expelled from an appalled German Chamber of Architects.

The production of cigarettes in the landmark building ceased in 1952. Cultural events now take place under Yenidze's 18-meter-high glass dome. The highest beer garden in Dresden is located on the roof of the magnificent monument and is a popular meeting place.

The **Royal Palace** was the seat of Saxony's electors and kings from 1547 to 1918. It is one of the oldest buildings in the city, and one on which various architectural styles have left their mark. Impressive Renaissance structures adorn the small and large courtyards, while the outer facades, created between 1889 and 1901, are in the Neo-Renaissance style with Baroque elements (previous double page). The monumental Hausmann Tower in the north wing dates from ca. 1400. It was given its Baroque spire in 1676 and, at 101 meters, is the highest tower in the city and surroundings.

A masterpiece of German Renaissance architecture is the palace's large courtyard, which was constructed between 1548 and 1556 under the direction of architect Caspar Voigt von Wieran. Stunning sgraffito painting adorns its facades (bottom left).

During World War II, the Royal Palace burned down to its founctions. The gradual reconstruction of individual rooms is ongoing The medieval palace chapel, with its Late Gothic vault (top le can once again be admired. The chapel's Renaissance gate, al called the "Beautiful Gate" or "Golden Gate," dates from 155 (top right).

The extensive Royal Palace is now an outstanding museum co plex. With its modern roof made of plastic diamond-shape elements, the Small Courtyard serves as a foyer for the museu complex (bottom right).

The **Armory** depicts chivalry from its most brilliant side. The Hall of the Giants in the Royal Palace is filled with sparkling armor and ornate weapons, which the Saxon rulers began collecting in the 15th century. These status symbols of the blue-blooded rulers were worn only on special occasions, such as tournaments and festive processions. Figures of knights equipped with armor and lances sit on splendidly decorated wooden horses, bringing the royal court culture back to life (above).

Among the highlights of the 350 exhibits is the splendid golden and silver armor for a man and his horse. This magnificent set of armor was crafted between 1562 and 1564 by the Antwerp goldsmith, Eliseus Libaerts, who had been commissioned by the Swedish King, Erik XIV (bottom left). One can also see three Saxon electoral swords, including that of the first Elector of Saxony, Friedrich I (1423–28).

The Armory is one of the largest collections of its kind. Since 2013, it has been located in the Hall of the Giants (bottom right), a Renaissance banquet hall, which was reconstructed in a new design. The largest hall in the palace is reached via the English Staircase, built in 1692.

Although the Saxon electors fought along the Habsburgs against the Ottoman invaders in southeastern Europe in the Turkish Wars of the 16th and 17th centuries, they had a weakness for richly decorated oriental arms and military equipment. Those who visit the exhibition in the Royal Palace's **Turkish Chamber** will share their enthusiasm for the magnificent crafts of the East. With nearly six hundred exhibits from the Electors' outstanding collections, this collection is one of the most important of its kind outside of Turkey.

On display are suits of armor, scimitars, daggers and guns, which are richly decorated with gold and precious stones (bottom right). Oriental accents also embellish the saddles and valaes, which adorn the life-sized horse figures (top right). The te in the collection are also impressive; this is especially true of t Ottoman state tent, which dates from the 17th century and whi is decorated with gold and silk (left). Another highlight in the c lection is the horse figure, which is clothed in a suit of metal armwhich was a common practice in the late 15th century in t Orient.

With a few exceptions, the exhibits were not war loot. Rather, th came into the collection after being acquired as diplomatic gifts as purchases made by the Saxon court.

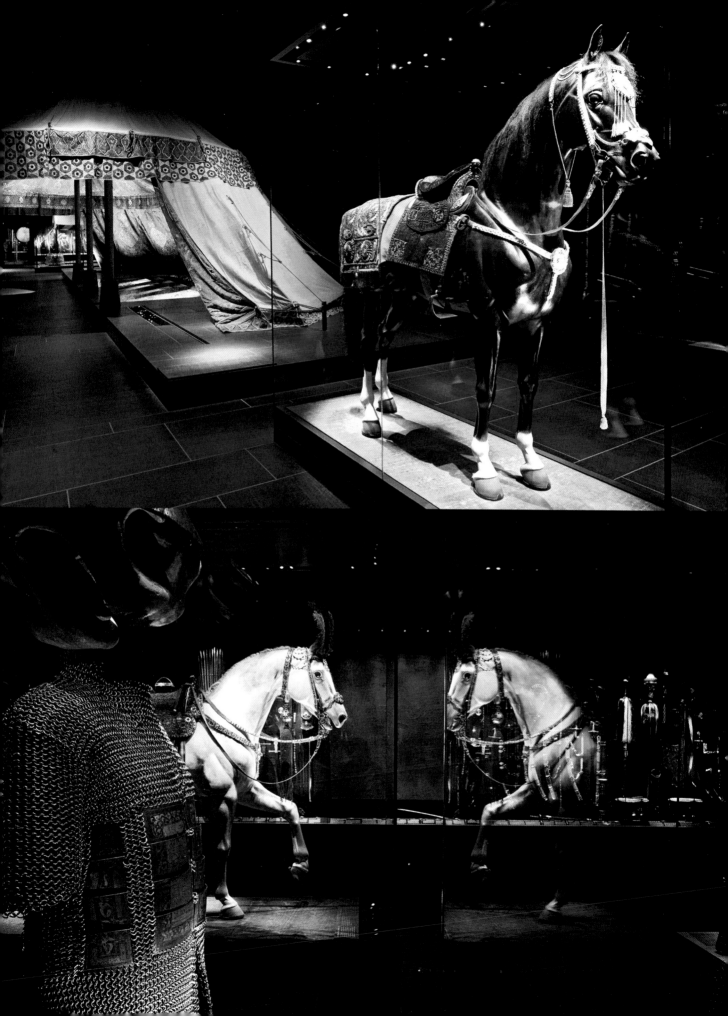

The highlight of the Royal Palace's collections is the Neues Grünes Gewölbe (New Green Vault) in the west wing, which is divided into the Neues Grünes Gewölbe, in which artworks are in the foreground, and the **Historisches Grünes Gewölbe** (Historic Green Vault), where exhibits are displayed in magnificent rooms with floor-to-ceiling mirrors and baroque consoles showing August the Strong's fondness for an ostentatious display of prestige.

The absolute ruler had the opulent Grünes Gewölbe constructed 1723–32 to house the electoral art treasures and present the wealth of the Wettiner to select guests. The museum character of the interior design was unusual for the time.

After years of restoration, since 2006, impressive and spectacular artwork from Saxony's most glamorous era has been displayed in the Historisches Grünes Gewölbe. More than two thousand art treasures and exquisite objects of gold, silver, precious stones, crystal, amber and ivory overwhelm the visitors in the luxurious Baroque setting. The White Silver Room, Silver Gilt Room (above), the Hall of Precious Objects, the Bronze and Jewel rooms (previous double page) were faithfully reconstructed. Balthasar Permoser's famous exotic "Moor with Emerald Cluster" from 1724 (below) is on view in the Jewel Room.

e Baroque wonders of the Historisches Grünes Gewölbe are
omplemented by the **Neues Grünes Gewölbe,** where more than
e thousand delicate artworks of the Wettiner treasury are pre-
nted in a modern way. The artworks here attest to the amazing
enius and often refined and detailed richness of Dresden's gold-
niths' and jewelers' art.

e work of the brilliant court jeweler Johann Melchior Dinglinger
664–1731) is presented in a separate hall. Works include the
olden coffee set for August the Strong (below). Executed in 1697,
e service includes 45 pieces made of gold, silver and enamel,
nd embellished with 5,600 diamonds. Fascinating is the stage-
e miniature of the "Court of Delhi on the Birthday of the Grand
ogul Aureng-Zeb" (following double page). This exotic fairy tale
orld inhabited by 137 colored enamel humans, horses and ele-
ants was designed by Dinglinger and created with 1701–08
ith the help of his brothers. August the Strong paid more for for
e miniature world of sparkling jewels and diamonds than for the
onstruction of Moritzburg Castle.

n ivory frigate created by the turner Jacob Zeller in 1620 for the
axon court is of breathtaking perfection (above). Tiny ivory sailors
imb the rigging of gold wire.

IV. AUGUST II. AUGUST III. FRIED
1694–1733. 1733–1763.

The Northern Renaissance style, which characterizes the Royal Palace, was enhanced by the beautiful proportions of the Italian Renaissance between 1586 and 1591, when the building was enlarged to include the **Long Colonnade** (bottom right).

The arcades formed by round arches and supported by twenty Tuscan columns along the courtyard, called the Stable Court, are perfect examples of Florentine architecture and were realized by Giovanni Maria Nosseni for Elector Christian I. The capitals are adorned with horns, antlers and coats of arms. The upper level is painted with vines, plants and grotesque figures.

40 Jousting tournaments and festivals were held in the Stable Court.

Two six-meter-high ornate bronze columns, designed by Nosse and used for casual ring jousting, are reminders of this.

The Procession of Princes (top right), a monumental mural on th Long Colonnade facing Augustusstrasse, depicts the Saxon rule – from Konrad the Great (1123–56) and August the Strong (to left) to King Friedrich August III (1904–18). The 102-meter-lon gallery of Wettiner ancestors was originally created by Wilhel Walther 1872–76 as sgraffito. In 1906/07 the Procession Princes was transferred onto Meissen porcelain. The porcelain m ral with 24,000 tiles survived the scorching flames of the Februar 1945 bombing raids.

With the construction of the Stable Court in the Royal Palace, an additional stable building, which formed the structural conclusion of the royal complex, the **Johanneum** (top right), was erected in 1586–90. The Renaissance building by Paul Buchner was rebuilt twice in the 18th century to accommodate the painting collection of the Saxon rulers. The functional structure received its palatial appearance between 1744 and 1746 from Johann Christoph Knöffel, who also preserved the original Renaissance portals. When the precious artworks were moved to the Gemäldegalerie in the Zwinger complex, the art-loving King Johann (1801–73), after whom the building was then named, transformed the structure into a history museum. After its war-related reconstruction began in 1950, the Johanneum's original role as a coach house was revived when, in 1956, it became the home of the Dresden Transport Museum.

On display in the museum are pioneer and vintage vehicles of the road (top left), railway and air. The steam locomotive "Muldenthal" from 1861 recalls Saxony's railway history. Also on view is the world's first three-phase experimental locomotive from 1899, as well as Saxony's oldest tram. In the courtyard are classics of Saxon and East German automotive history (bottom left).

Animated exhibits in the family-friendly museum give everyone the opportunity to be a captain or pilot (bottom right).

Bruehl Terrace, located high above the Elbe on the city's fortifications in Dresden's Old Town (previous double page), was discovered by Count Heinrich von Brühl (1700–63). Beginning in 1737, Saxony's prime minister and closest confidante of Elector Friedrich August II had a series of Baroque palaces built on the former bulwark. In 1814, half a century after Brühl's death, it was opened to the public, and a monumental staircase, designed by Friedrich Gottlob Thor Meyer, was built on the Palace Square. Since then, strollers from all over the world have been drawn to the "Balcony of Europe," where they enjoy the unique harmony between the city and river. In the 19th century, Brühl's Baroque buildings gradually gave way to the magnificent structures that now line the world famous promenade.

At the western entrance, directly adjacent to the staircase, y_ will find the Saxon Ständehaus, built between 1901 and 190_ (bottom left). The historical seat of the Saxon Parliament, it w_ designed by Paul Wallot, the architect of the Berlin Reichstag. It stands next to the Sekundogenitur house, erected in 1897 (t_ right). The Neo-Baroque facade of the cafe is based on that of _ original Bruehl Palace.

Located directly to the east of the terrace is the magnificent co_ plex of the Academy of Fine Arts, also called the Lipsiusbau (t_ left). Architect Konstantin Lipsius crowned the ensemble, erect_ between 1887 and 1894, with a glass dome. The monume_ dedicated to the Romantic painter Ludwig Richter (1803–84) h_ once again stood in front of the building since 2013 (bottom righ_

Bruehl Terrace rests on the city's old fortifications. The fortress that once surrounded the city was designed by Caspar Voigt von Wierandt for Elector Moritz, who reigned from 1546 to 1556. In 1590, an additional bastion was built along the Elbe River near the present Albertinum. This part of the Renaissance complex is known as the **Dresden Fortress** (above). Besides casemates, canon courtyards, ramparts and watch rooms, it houses the oldest remaining gate in Dresden, the Brick Gate, dating from around 1550.

The Moritz Monument, which is situated on the corner of the bastion facing the Elbe, also dates from this same period (below). The copy of the oldest monument in Dresden recalls the violent death of the owner of the fortress in 1553; the sculpture – created by sculptor Hans Walther II in 1555 – depicts the Saxon ruler Moritz passing the electoral sword to his brother August.

In 1708, in the stone vaults of the fortress, naturalists and alchemists Johann Friedrich Böttger and Walther von Tschirnhaus took notes as they manufactured porcelain for the first time in Europe. August the Strong had interned the supposed gold-makers in the hopes of filling his empty coffers.

The **Albertinum** (above) forms the eastern end of Bruehl Terrace. The lavish ornamentation on the facade, which was added when the building was remodeled between 1884 and 1887, reveals that it is a temple for art. The idea was that this would help the people of Dresden to get used to the building's new function; until then it had been used as a weapons depot for more than three centuries.

The historic Armory, built between 1559 and 1563 according to plans of the court architect Caspar Voigt von Wierandt, was one of the most magnificent Renaissance structures in Dresden. It was also one of the largest armories in Europe. The vaults of the vaunted arsenal are preserved on the ground floor.

The reconstruction of the museum at the end of the 19th century was carried out by the architect Karl Adolf Canzler in the style of the Italian High Renaissance. The building bears the name of King Albert, who ruled over the Saxons at that time.

After the great flood of 2002, measures were taken to protect the Albertinum from future flood damage. Seventeen meters above the courtyard is a two-storey depot for the valuable art treasures of the museum's New Masters Gallery and its sculpture collection. The covered courtyard serves as an exhibition hall for the museum (below).

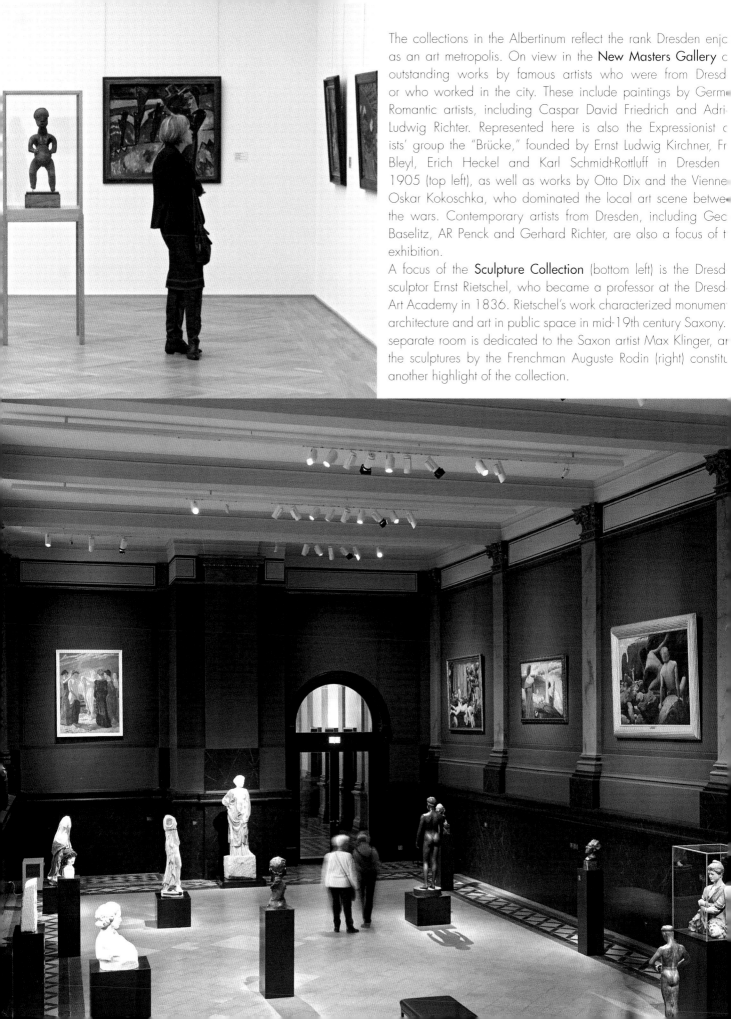

The collections in the Albertinum reflect the rank Dresden enjc as an art metropolis. On view in the **New Masters Gallery** c outstanding works by famous artists who were from Dresd or who worked in the city. These include paintings by Germe Romantic artists, including Caspar David Friedrich and Adri Ludwig Richter. Represented here is also the Expressionist c ists' group the "Brücke," founded by Ernst Ludwig Kirchner, Fr Bleyl, Erich Heckel and Karl Schmidt-Rottluff in Dresden 1905 (top left), as well as works by Otto Dix and the Vienne Oskar Kokoschka, who dominated the local art scene betwee the wars. Contemporary artists from Dresden, including Gec Baselitz, AR Penck and Gerhard Richter, are also a focus of t exhibition.

A focus of the **Sculpture Collection** (bottom left) is the Dresd sculptor Ernst Rietschel, who became a professor at the Dresd Art Academy in 1836. Rietschel's work characterized monumen architecture and art in public space in mid-19th century Saxony. separate room is dedicated to the Saxon artist Max Klinger, ar the sculptures by the Frenchman Auguste Rodin (right) constitu another highlight of the collection.

Located where the Bruehl Terrace ends by the river is the **New Synagogue** (below). This religious structure, which was consecrated in 2001, stands on the historic site of the Old Synagogue, which was set on fire during Kristallnacht in 1938 and later demolished. It, like the town hall opposite it, was designed by the Saarbrücken architects Wandel, Hoefer, Lorch and Hirsch.

In the New Synagogue, traditional elements of Jewish worship are united with a contemporary architectural structure, which has won several awards. The synagogue's 24-meter-high cube-shaped construction recalls the Temple of Solomon. In order for the building to face east, in spite of the narrow plot on which it stands, the windowless facade shifts, layer by thin layer, in the required direction. In the simple sanctuary, a fine golden metal fabric symbolizes the tabernacle, the center of Jewish worship during the time the Jews wandered through the desert (above).

The Star of David at the entrance was rescued from the Old Synagogue, which was consecrated in 1840 and designed by Gottfried Semper. Broken glass in the ground depicts the floor plan of the original, destroyed synagogue.

addition to its much-vaunted art treasures, Dresden also offers different kind of pastime for tourists: the oldest fleet of **Paddle Steamers** in the world. Nine historical ships, which are now owned by the Saxon Steamship Company, are docked along Bruehl Terrace (top photograph).

The oldest of these snow-white steamers was launched in 1879. Originally christened "Dresden III," today the methuselah cruises leisurely across the Elbe River and now bears the more cosmopolitan name, "Stadt Wehlen."

As in the days of the Kaiser, the nostalgic excursion ships are propelled forward by paddle wheels located in the lateral wheel housings and are driven by steam engines. One of the original machines is still fired with coal.

Guests on the Paddle Steamers can enjoy Dresden at its very best. The boats travel up the Elbe, along the scenic Elbe palisades (below), on past the bridge, the Blue Wonder in Loschwitz, and farther up to Pillnitz Castle; travelling downriver leads to the historic town of Meissen.

Dresden owes its fame as a Baroque city not only to its nobility's desire for grandeur. Even the proud bourgeoisie felt an affinity towards architecture that reflected its social status. Evidence of this can once again be admired on **New Market Square**. Through the reconstruction of the Old Town according to the historical model, in recent years bourgeois Dresden has been reconstructed here and in the surrounding streets, and once again shines in its former glory.

Magnificent Baroque facades with cheerful Rococo ornamentation were faithfully reconstructed. Among the most treasured replicas are the Köhler House with its Rococo gateway, at the corner of Frauenstrasse, originally built in 1749, and the Heinrich Schü residence from 1731 at New Market 12 (bottom right). The latte building was designed by George Bähr, who was also the arch tect of the Frauenkirche. Bähr also drew up the plans for the state Hotel de Saxe, located on the square (bottom left), and a cit palace in Landhausstrasse, which was rebuilt as the British Hotel The monument in front of the Hotel de Saxe depicts King Friedric August II, who gave the Saxons a constitution in 1831. The statu of the reformer Martin Luther, in the center of New Market Squar (above), was unveiled in 1885. The oldest artwork on the squar is the Turkish fountain from the year 1648.

The **Frauenkirche** (Church of Our Lady) dominates the silhouette of the Old Town and is a Dresden landmark. The church on New Market Square is one of the greatest Baroque monuments in Europe (right). Its bell-shaped sandstone dome is an architectural feat. The architect of this unique church was George Bähr (1666–1738), who became the city's master carpenter in 1705. The Protestant church was built between 1726 and 1743 as an expression of Dresden's confident civic community. With its lantern, the church rises 91 meters into the sky. Via a spiral ramp, visitors reach the observation deck located at 67 meters.

The circular nave with its four-storey colorfully painted galleries and the Late Baroque altar (previous double page) are impressive. A ceiling painting on the cupola's interior depicts the four evange-

lists (bottom right) and was executed by Giovanni Battista Gror (1682–1748).

After three air raids on Dresden, the burned-out Frauenkirch collapsed on the morning of February 15, 1945. Only the m sonry of the chancel and an adjacent stair tower remained stan ing (top left). The wish of Dresden's citizens to reconstruct th city's landmark structure was fulfilled following the reunification Germany. In 1993, the meticulous "archaeological clearance" the rubble at the base of the church ruins began (bottom lef Reconstructed according to original plans, a quarter of the churc consists of original material. On 30 October, 2005, the churc was consecrated, and is once again one of the most magnifice Protestant churches in Europe.

The most elegant Baroque structure near the Frauenkirche is th
bright yellow **Cosel Palace** (above). This magnificent urban vill
was built in 1765 for Friedrich August von Cosel, the product c
the glamorous liaison between August the Strong and his mo
famous mistress, Countess Anna Constanze von Cosel.

The architectural gem of Dresden's aristocracy was faithfully recor
structed between 1998 and 2000. Only the low side wing an
the stately fence at the main courtyard survived the Second Worl
War. The militaristic ornamentation recalled that the noble landlor
fought in the Seven Years' War as a Saxon general. The courtyar
is embellished with a beautiful wall fountain.

Today the building attracts visitors with its excellent cuisine in lu:
urious surroundings. The Grand Café seduces with Dresdner spe
cialties (below). Located in the vaulted basement of the palace i
the restaurant Pulverturm, where visitors can dine surrounded b
medieval masonry.

Another excellent culinary venue is housed in Kurländer Palace, lo
cated behind Cosel Palace on Tzschirner Square. The building wa
built in 1729 according to plans of Johann Christoph Knöffel who
as Saxony's chief master builder, left his stamp on Baroque Dresden

ot far from New Market Square is an attraction that attests to
xony's history. The Late Baroque **Landhaus** (below) on the epon-
nous street was the meeting place of Saxon's provincial diet from
'75 to 1907. Because this committee was responsible for the
xation of the electorate, it is regarded as a forerunner of today's
ate parliament. In 1907 the Ständehaus (Assembly Hall) on Pal-
e Square took over this function.

is stately villa, whose main facade was executed in the
assical style, was designed by the court architect, Friedrich
ugust Krubsacius. An elegantly curved double-staircase with
coco elements adorns the entrance hall (above). A newer stair-
se, which was built to serve the villa's current use as the home
the Municipal Art Gallery, also attracts attention: an exterior,
tistically distorted emergency staircase leading to Pirnaischer
quare.

e place in which Saxony's finances were once controlled is now
edicated to the art and cultural history of the city. In addition to
esden's major art collections, since 1965 the villa has been
ome to the Dresden City Museum, where over eight hundred
ars of history are on view.

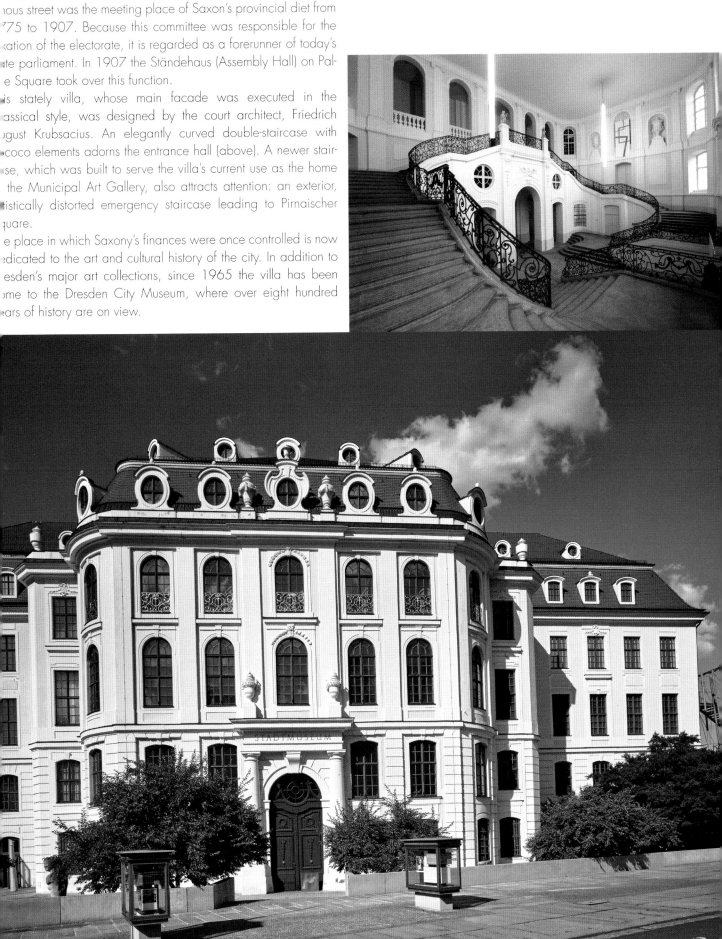

The **Dresden City Museum** in the Landhaus informs visitors about Dresden's often turbulent history. The rise of Dresden began when the Albertine line of the House of Wettin made this site on the river Elbe its royal seat in 1485. The exhibited wooden panel painting "The Ten Commandments" on view is an important testimony from that period. The cycle was painted 1528/29 by Johann (Hans).

Many testimonies of the past recovered from the rubble of World War II can be seen in the Dresden City Museum, such as the head of a statue, which once stood on Old Market Square (top left), and architectural ornamentation of the destroyed Gothic church

St. Sophia. A model of the city shows its Baroque center arou the Frauenkirche (top right). Various everyday objects recall t time of the GDR (below).

The holdings of city's own art collection, established in 186 constitute the basis of what is now the **Dresden City Art Museu** The present collection focuses on 20th century and contempor Dresden. Among the local artists who are represented with wo in the collection are Otto Dix, Thoralf Knobloch and AR Pen The graphic collection is also outstanding and includes the old known image of Dresden, which dates from 1570 and is the wo of Gabriel Tola.

Familie
Unser Zuhause

PRAMO

The **Old Market Square** was once the mercantile heart of Dresden. The oldest square in this city on the Elbe was first mentioned in 1370. The square we see today is several times larger than the original and a creation of the 20th century, a place where buildings from the postwar period set the tone. The facades along the east and west side of the square date from 1953 to 1958, and reflect local building traditions (bottom left, right half of the picture). Architects Alexander Künzer, Johannes Rascher and Herbert Schneider adorned the facades without completely abandoning the Baroque style. Under the arcades, stores emerged, whose lively interiors reflect the optimism of the 1950s.

The Palace of Culture opened in 1969 on the northern side the Old Market Square and broke with the city's architectu past (above). The heroic mural "The Path of the Red Flag" alo Schossstrasse recalls the GDR's communist era. The functional f structure houses the Dresden Philharmonic's new concert hall. Where the winding streets of the medieval town center once stoo stands Dresden's largest shopping mall. The expansive Old Mark Gallery (bottom right) is concealed behind the west front of t rectangular square. There the confectionery Kreutzkamm, whi has been located on the Old Market Square since 1825, serv and sells its famous pyramid cake.

ery year, in late November, the Old Market Square is transmed into an impressive Christmas market. The **Striezelmarkt** as first mentioned in 1434 and is Germany's oldest market of e Advent season. Thanks to the village-like design of the approxately 250 stands, a cozy atmosphere is guaranteed despite the owds (below). Children in particular will find what their hearts sire.

e market was named after Dresden's most famous pastry: iezel, the original name of stollen, which was sold during the e-Christmas Advent period. In 1491, Pope Innocent VIII even essed the use of the nutrient-rich ingredients butter and milk. On e Second Sunday of Advent, the people of Dresden pay tribute their world-famous cake and local bakers present a one-ton ant stollen at the Stollen Festival.

addition to the many treats is the 14-meter-high step pyramid m the Erzgebirge that includes 42 wooden figures and is one of e Striezelmarkt's greatest attractions (above).

owadays, during the Advent period, all of Dresden is transmed into a single Christmas market. Nostalgic stands are also cated in the Stable Courtyard and around the Frauenkirche.

Kreuzkirche (Church of the Holy Cross) is the only building on Old Market Square that pre-dates World War II (below). Founded in 1200, it owes its name to a fragment of the True Cross given to the church in 1234 and kept here as a relic. In its 800-year history, Dresden's largest church was repeatedly destroyed and rebuilt. The present sandstone church dates from 1764–88.

The construction of a new building was necessary because the older sacred structure had been destroyed by the bombardments of Prussian troops in 1760 during the Seven Years' War. The painter Canaletto captured the depressing sight of the ruins in one of his works. The church's reconstruction by three architects resulted in a mixture of styles ranging from Baroque to Classic. The accessible tower is 92 meters high.

The opulent interior fell victim to fire in 1897 and 1945. In the chancel remnants of Art Nouveau elements from the early 1900's been preserved (above). Bare plaster dominates the rest of the building. The bells survived all these events undamaged and are among the largest in Germany.

The internationally famous Dresdner Kreuzchor, a traditional boys' choir with 150 members, dates back to ca. 1300 and is part of the Kreuzschule, which Richard Wagner attended.

The view from Dresden's City Hall, southeast of Old Market Square, over the ruins of the completely-destroyed town is an eternal reminder of its past. The world-famous photo from 1945 was taken from the almost 100-meter-high tower, which had survived the firestorm of bombing raids in February. The gilded Rathausmann on the spire also survived with minimal damage. The 4,90-meter-high giant cornucopia embodies Hercules, who is patron of the city. After the war, the sculpture was granted landmark status.

The **New Town Hall** was built between 1905 and 1910 behind the Kreuzkirche. In the 1960s a modern ballroom wing was added to the building (above). The grand staircase hall with the monumental Art Nouveau ceiling painting by Otto Gussmann (below) is also impressive.

The New Garment House on the Town Hall Square was erected between 1768 and 1770, replacing the draper's old residence in New Market Square, which had been destroyed during the Seven Years' War. The simple Baroque building is now an elegant hotel, at the rear of which is a lovely sandstone fountain created in 1718, probably the work of the famous goldsmith, Johann Melchior Dinglinger.

Prager Strasse represents a contrast to Dresden's Baroque ci[ty] center. This traditional shopping street is a prime example of inte[r]national post-war Modernism. In the mid-1960s, it was created [as] an expansive pedestrian thoroughfare and is flanked by a row [of] hotels and a 240-meter-long block of flats.

The 1972 black and white striped round cinema on the nort[h]ern end is an architectural monument from the communist era (to[p] right). The crystal-shaped Ufa Cinema Center, built 1993 an[d] 1998, is adjacent to the original movie theater (bottom right). Th[is] extraordinary building was designed by the renowned Viennes[e] architectural firm Coop Himmelb(l)au.

Another highlight of modern architecture is the Centrum Galle[rie] (bottom left). Established in 2010, the shopping center is dec[o]rated with an extravagant facade consisting of 3,400 sculptur[ed] aluminum honeycombs, which were taken from the building th[at] had formerly stood on this spot. The Pusteblumen Fountain (top le[ft] and Völkerfreundschaft sculpture date from the time of the GDR[.] Prager Strasse leads to the main train station, which was inaug[u]rated in 1898. Since 2006, a Teflon roof, designed by Britis[h] architect Sir Norman Foster, has spanned the three platform hall[.]

The construction of the **Palace in the Great Garden** (bottom left) ushered in Dresden's greatest period as a Baroque city. After the Thirty Years War, Elector Johann Georg III (1647–91) commissioned a summer palace to be built outside the city's walls. Architect Johann Georg Starcke modeled his work on French chateaux and Italian villas and, in 1678–83, created one of the earliest Baroque structures in Central Europe. The palace is situated at the intersection of the Great Garden's two main axes.

In front of the palace stands the marble sculpture "Time Kidnaps Beauty," carved by the Italian Pietro Balestra in the 18th century. A typical Baroque composition is the "Üppigkeitsvase" by Antonio Corradini, situated along the palace pond (top right).

The Great Garden, created in 1676 together with the Palace to the east of the Old Town, was expanded to its present size under August the Strong. Karl Friedrich Bouché transformed the original Baroque garden into a landscaped park in 1676. With its 147 hectares, the Great Garden is the largest park of Dresden. The Botanical and Zoological Gardens are located in the complex. The cafe in Carolaschlösschen on Carola Lake (top left) invites guests to linger.

Another major attraction, for both children and adults, is the park railway, which meanders leisurely through the green oasis (bottom right). Two miniature steam locomotives from 1925 pull the narrow gauge railroad trains.

The **German Hygiene Museum** is the result of the life's work of the entrepreneur Karl August Lingner (1861–1916). The physical well-being of the population was a labor of love for the entrepreneur. Having made his fortune with the invention of the mouthwash "Odol," Lingner became actively engaged in the fight against endemic diseases and a promoter of preventative healthcare. On his initiative, the first International Hygiene Exhibition took place in Dresden in 1911. The large number of visitors encouraged the pharmaceutical industrialist – with the goal of educating the public on health care – to establish in 1912 the German Hygiene Museum, which moved into its present location along the Great Garden (top left) in 1930.

The unique concept of the institution offers a fascinating and entertaining adventure through the human body, but is also dedicated to themes such as nutrition and sexuality (bottom right, bottom left). Nearly 1300 exhibits are waiting to be discovered in the Neo-Classical building. A highlight of the exhibition is the "Transparent Woman" (right). The life-size dummy illustrates the inner workings of the human body and shows all its vessels, organs and bones.

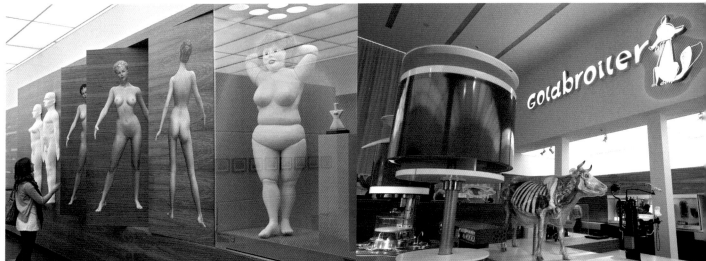

The **New Town Center** is a creation of the Baroque period and was built on the site of Old Dresden, which had been destroyed in a fire in 1685. The symmetrical network of streets for the new development on the northern banks of the Elbe was laid out by Wolf Caspar von Klengel. Located on the Königstrasse it is the only original preserved Baroque ensemble of townhouses in Dresden. As specified by the architect Matthäus Daniel Pöppelmann, elegant bourgeois townhouses began to be erected here in 1730. The Dreikönigskirche (Three Kings Church), consecrated in 1739, was a collaborative work by Pöppelmann and George Bähr (bottom left). The 87-meter-high tower made of sandstone was added in 1857.

The many passages that run through the buildings' courtyards contribute to the pleasant atmosphere of the New Town. Attractive shops and restaurants are enticing with their exquisite produc (bottom right).

On New Market Square (top left) there is an impressive symbol o the Augustan age, the glorious era of Dresden under Elector Augu the Strong and Friedrich August II: The Golden Rider (right) embod ies the power and political ambitions and the lavish splendor of th regents who formed Dresden into the impressive Baroque city it be came. The gilded equestrian statue depicts August the Strong as Roman emperor in scaled armor dar. The sculpture by Jean Josep Vinache was only completed in 1736 after the elector's death.

Dresden was not only a stronghold of the Baroque, but also center of the Romantic. The **Museum of Dresden Romanticism** Hauptstrasse in the New Town is dedicated to this important artic era. Remembrance is paid to the great minds who worked Dresden between 1785 and 1830: the painters Caspar Dav Friedrich, Carl Gustav Carus and Philipp Otto Runge; the compers Robert Schumann and Carl Maria von Weber; and the write ETA Hoffmann, Heinrich von Kleist and Novalis.

The museum is housed in the former home of the painter Gerha von Kügelgen (1772–1820). Among the early Romantic compoer's guests were many famous members of Dresden's art scen Kügelgen's studio has been reconstructed on the second floor (blow). In 1820, the professor of history painting was killed durir a robbery. His violent death shook the city on the Elbe.

The Kügelgenhaus is a typical townhouse of the New Town. Bu from 1697 to 1699, it received its current appearance betwee 1765 and 1770. Noteworthy are the preserved ceiling paintin from this period (above). The historic monument is one of the fe original buildings on the Hauptstrasse, the at times forty-meter-wic central axis of the Baroque New Town.

August the Strong, a lover of white gold, had had his way, Dresden would include another treasure – a palace with rooms covered in porcelain. To this end, he had the **Japanese Palace** (above) built in the New Town on the banks of the Elbe by his favorite architects, Matthäus Daniel Pöppelmann, Jean de Bodt and Zacharias Longuelune, between 1728 and 1733. The palace had Oriental-styled roofs and a portico reminiscent of the Louvre. Twenty-four jovial Chinese figures adorn the courtyard and contribute to the Asian character of the structure.

When the porcelain palace remained a mere dream, Friedrich August III (1750–1827) transformed the Japanese Palace between 1782 and 1786 into a museum, which announces its existence with the inscription "Museum Usui publico patens" (museum for public use). Several scientific exhibitions are on view in the palace today. The **Hunting Lodge** in the nearby Köpckestrasse has been dedicated to Saxon Folk Art for more than a century (bottom left). The Renaissance-style building was erected in 1617 and is the only remaining wing of the original electoral hunting lodge. On display here, among others things, is an exceptional and unique collection of dolls (bottom right).

For a hundred years, a military museum has been located in Dresden's Albertstadt district. In a time when armed conflict overshadowed world politics, the **Military History Museum** (below) took a critical look at the consequences for those affected by war. "Suffering in War" and "Politics and Violence" are topics addressed in the Militärhistorisches Museum der Bundeswehr, which opened in 2011. The use of "animals in the military" is also vividly depicted (top right).

The building's form illustrates the ambivalent character of the presented subject matter. Like an aggressive gesture, a sharp metal wedge breaks through the main facade of the old arsenal from the Imperial era. The wedge is the most striking element of building's renovation (2003–11) by the American architect Dar Libeskind, whose architectural style has created unusual museum spaces. A view of Dresden can be enjoyed from the buildin spectacular tip. The Neo-Classical building from 1875 was p of a vast complex of barracks.

The exhibition provides information on the history and operatic of the Bundeswehr and recalls the National People's Army of GDR. On view is historical military equipment, such as a subm rine, built in 1851. Weapons, uniforms, guns and large comb vehicles are also on display (top left).

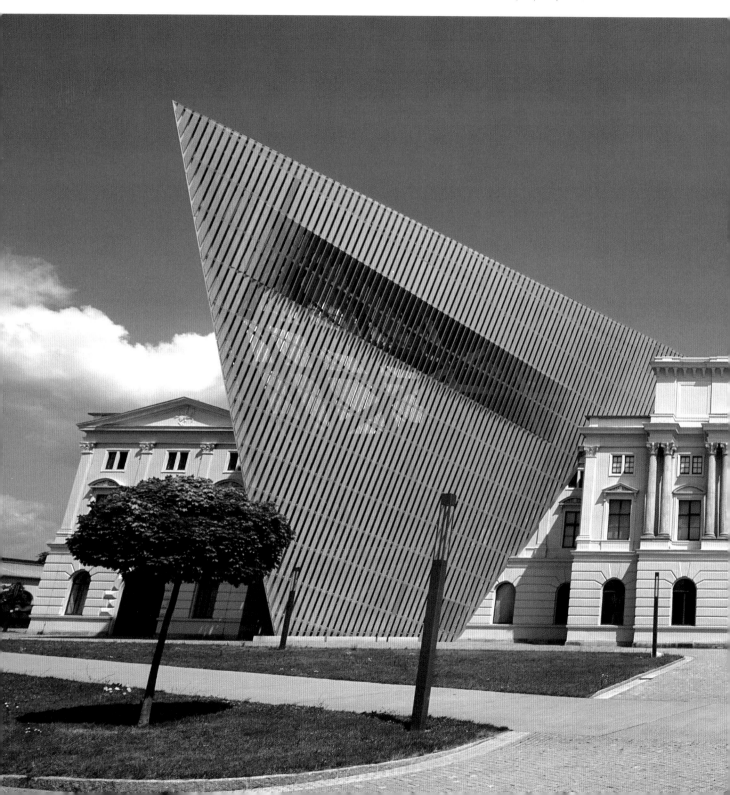

Only in Dresden could a dairy shop become a place of pilgrimage. With everything from amazement to reverence, visitors from around the world come to see the colorful walls and ceilings of **Pfunds Molkerei** (Pfund's Dairy Store). The overwhelming decoration consisting of 3,500 majolica tiles made its way into the Guinness Book of Records, an honor which the Pfund brothers did not have in mind when, in 1892, they commissioned their dairy shop to be decorated by the Dresdner ceramics company Villeroy & Boch (above).

The tiles depict the world of milk production, and visitors can gaze at images of grazing cows, butterflies, mythical creatures and cheerful cherubs and angels. The sumptuous ornamental work of the hand-painted tiles, the ornate columns and the elegant fountain give the store the dreamlike atmosphere of a magnificent palatial hall.

Hygienic milk is no longer the main product sold here, as it was in the days of Paul Gustav Pfund (1849–1923), but rather, a rich variety of cheeses (below). A café is located on the upper floor.

sense for tasteful urban spaces continues to be particularly pronounced in Dresden. One example is the **Kunsthof Arcade** in the Outer New Town, hidden behind the late 19th century facades on Alaunstrasse and Görlitzer Strasse.

In the five courtyards one finds an unusual mixture of imaginative facades, exceptional shops and original craftwork. In ca. 2000, every courtyard was given an individual appearance.

The Courtyard of the Mythical Creatures was adorned with fantastical figures depicted in mosaics by artist Viola Schöpe (below). In the Courtyard of the Metamorphoses one finds building-high steel sculptures; in the Courtyard of Light, metal mirrors create a flickering light show. A much-visited attraction is the Courtyard of the Elements, where water and sun are the focus. On one side of a bright yellow building golden plates flicker. On the sky-blue wall opposite this is a rain drainage system, created out of an attractive network of hoppers, gutters and downspouts (above). In the Courtyard of the Animals there are sandstone reliefs of cranes, monkeys and giraffes; and a lime green wall with balconies made of wicker.

The Outer New Town north of Albert Square is one of Dresden's trendy districts.

While looking for a location for his new home, a Prussian aristocrat discovered the beautiful site along the banks of the Elbe to the east of Dresden's center. Prince Albrecht of Prussia (1809–72) had to leave his home state because of his "improper marriage." In 1854, he moved into his new residence, Albrechtsberg Palace, named after him (top left). The building's exposed position, monumental structure and imposing terrace complex recall Roman Renaissance palaces. Albrecht's asylum resembles a triumphal gesture of defiance. The couple had one hundred rooms at their disposal, including the magnificent Crown Hall.

The palace's architect Adolf Lohse, a student of Friedrich Schinkel, simultaneously designed the neighboring villa for Marshal Bar[e] von Stockhausen. The building is known as Lingnerschloss (t[o] right), because the Odol inventor Karl August Lingner acquire[d] in 1906. At the foot of the vineyard, along the banks of the Elb[e] is an Art Nouveau mausoleum, designed by Hans Poelzig for t[he] owner, Lingner, who died in 1916.

The picturesque pearl necklace **Elbe Palaces** end with E[c]berg Palace (below), which was built in the English Tudor sty[le] in 1859–61 for the merchant John Daniel Souchay. The ne[o] Gothic palace, designed by the Semper-student Christian Frie[d]rich Arnold, is now a luxury hotel.

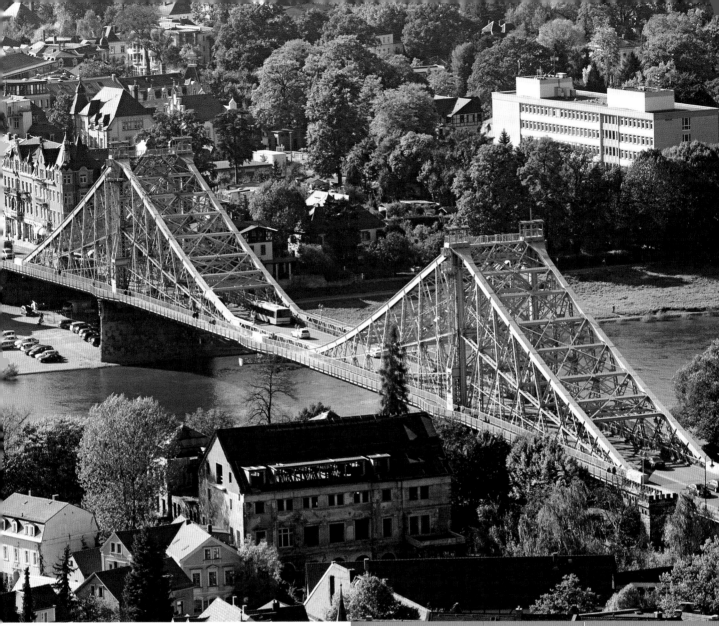

The Loschwitz Bridge (below) dates back to a time when engineers wowed people with their stunning works. When it was inaugurated in 1893, it was a technical sensation for Dresden, comparable to the unveiling of the Eiffel Tower four years earlier in Paris. The **Blue Wonder** has since been the name of the delicate bridge made of riveted steel trusses, which spans the river picturesquely between Blasewitz and Loschwitz (above). The fact it could cross high above the 140-meter-wide river bed without any supporting pillars was a novelty back then.

Because the authorities had an uneasy feeling about the progressive structure, before opening the turquoise bridge, they conducted a foolhardy safety test. Steamrollers weighing up to several tons and tram lorries full of rocks rolled over the 270-meter-long Elbe crossing. Even a fully-occupied tramcar, a company of soldiers and around 150 volunteers were sent over the bridge in a risky test meant to verify the structure's safety.

The Blue Wonder survived the Second World War because courageous individuals sabotaged the German Army's plans to blow it up in the final days of the war. Trams continued to roll over the bridge until 1986.

The idyllic **Loschwitz** district (below) has preserved much of its charm as a former wine-producing village. Friedrich Schiller was still able to enjoy the vineyards during his time in Dresden from 1785 to 1787. The poet liked retreating to the vineyard garden house of his friend, Christian Gottfried Körner, to write. Now known as the "Schillerhäuschen," it is a reminder of the poet's sojourn in Loschwitz. One hundred years later, the vines on the river slopes were abandoned, and Loschwitz was transformed into a popular residential area.

Another attraction is the picturesque, half-timbered farmstead of Eduard Leonhardi (1828–1905), who was a student of the romantic artist, Ludwig Richter. The artist's residence in the Grundstrasse is now home to the Leonhardi Museum, where works by its namesake are on view (top left).

The ascent from the center to the elegant residential areas on banks of the Elbe can be very easily made using the Loschwitz niculars: two sets of this unique form of transportation, both of whi date from ca. 1900, arouse feelings of nostalgia. One funicul built in 1895, starts its ascent on Körner Square. The route of t second historic cable car starts to the east of Körner Square. This hicle is a monorail, which, unlike the Wuppertal suspension railwo can make steep uphill climbs (top right). Since 1901, this first cak car in the world has overcome the 84-meter height difference. viewing platform is located at the station on top of the mountain

Pillnitz Castle on the Elbe is, like the Zwinger, a masterpiece created by the great architect Matthäus Daniel Pöppelmann. August the Strong commissioned Pöppelmann to design two Chinese palaces with cheerful lilting roofs and picturesque chimneys. The red-orange facades are embellished with murals with Chinese motifs.

The Oriental-looking ensemble, consisting of the Water Palace (above) and its mirror image, the Mountain Palace (previous double page), was built between 1720 and 1724 next to an older palace, which the monarch had given to his mistress, Countess Cosel. After she fell out of favor, the elector used the complex located in what is now the eastern outskirts of Dresden for his fes-

tivities. Splendid gondolas dropped off boisterous courtiers at the foot of the grand outdoor staircase.

Following a fire, the Cosel residence was replaced by the New Palace (bottom right), which connected the Water and Mountain Palaces. The Classical building designed by Christian Friedrich Schuricht was erected between 1818 and 1826.

The first trees in the Pillnitz Castle Park were planted by the Countess of Cosel. In the Countess' garden there is a reconstructed Baroque gondola with a carved figurehead (bottom left) like the one used by members of the court for their festive boat trips to Pillnitz. The park was further developed in the style of an English landscape garden beginning in 1778.

It is worth visiting the two museums in Pillnitz Castle: the Museum of Decorative Arts, housed here since 1962, and the Castle Museum.

The **Museum of Decorative Arts** in the Water and Mountain Palaces presents an interesting overview of noble interior design from the Middle Ages to the present. Among the exhibited furniture are precious gilded audience chairs from the time of August the Strong (bottom left). Renaissance cabinets amaze us with their expert craftsmanship. Other exhibits include French furniture, Italian majolica, Delftware, noble fabrics from Europe and the Orient and fine ceramics, forging and precious metals. Highlights are authentically styled rooms with Baroque chinoiserie and elegant Early Classical décor. Pioneering furniture from the turn of the century manufactured by the Deutsche Werkstätten Hellerau in Dresden and the Dresden art nouveau movement are also on view (top right).

The New Palace houses the **Castle Museum**, which vividly traces the history of the palace and life in the Saxon court. The New Classical ceiling and wall paintings are impressive. The kitchen area (bottom right) reveals many culinary secrets. The Catholic Chapel (top left) is a popular setting for festive wedding ceremonies.

hen the Saxon court went hunting, it traveled 15 kilometers north
Dresden to the **Moritzburg Hunting Lodge**. These noblemen's
ssion for hunting is in part thanks to this magnificent Baroque
ing, the center of which is Moritzburg Castle (top right). Four
cular towers, arranged in a square, stand on an artificial island,
d rise up from the lake below.

e building was created between 1723 and 1733, under the
ection of Matthäus Daniel Pöppelmann, who reconstructed the
ctoral castle from the Renaissance period. The magnificent
apel by Wolf Caspar von Klengel, built between 1661 and
572, was incorporated in the new ensemble.

riving at the castle one is greeted by sandstone piqueurs blowing
nting horns (left). August the Strong, the building's owner, lived to
e his ambitious building project completed. Friedrich August III
ded a Rococo jewel to the royal grounds in 1776: The Little
easant Castle, which was designed by Johann Daniel Schade,
he smallest palace built by the Saxon crown (bottom right). The
arm of the rose-colored gem, situated two and a half kilometers
st of the main castle, is irresistible. The often tiny rooms contain
any of Saxony's precious Rococo furnishings.

August the Strong was known for his extravagance. A prime example is the Feather Room (above) in the **Moritzburg Castle Museum**. The canopy for his bed and the curtains are made of more than one million feathers. The brightly patterned individual pieces were produced in 1720 in London and originally used in the Japanese Palace.

The original furnishings of the former Moritzburg Hunting Lodge include one of the most important collections of hunting trophies in Europe. Countless red deer antlers decorate the walls of the large Stone Hall (bottom left) and the Hall of Monstrosities (bottom right).

Unique is the extensive collection of leather wallpaper, whic adorns eleven rooms and which is mostly painted in the Baroq style. Many designs were created by the court painter Louis Silvestre of Paris (1675–1760).

Another highlight is the historical porcelain collection housed the Hunting Tower, one of the castle's four round towers. Son of the more than one hundred exhibits come from China and J pan, but most were made in the manufactory in Meissen ar date from the 18th century. The figurines represent animals ar hunting scenes, such as an impressive bison engaged in a fig with boars.

Index of Sights

ustrations
side front cover: Royal Palace, Large Courtyard
3: Zwinger, Rampart Pavilion

opyright photos
ok | Staatliche Kunstsammlungen Dresden | Elke Estel: p. 8f.
ndesarchiv: p. 5 bottom (Alfred Frankl), 6f., 7 top left (Hahn),
top right (Ugo Proietti), 58 top (Ugo Proietti)
rary of Congress Washington: p. 4, 5 top
esse- und Informationsamt der Bundesregierung: p. 58 bottom left
ühler)
l other photographs: Günter Schneider

Original edition
1st edition 2015
© 2015 Jaron Verlag GmbH, Berlin
(Original title: "Faszinierendes Dresden. Elbflorenz in prächtigen Fotografien")
All rights reserved. Any use of this work – even in part – is only permitted
with permission from the publisher. This especially applies for duplications,
translation, microfilms, other types of processing, as well as for the storing
and processing in electronic systems.
www.jaron-verlag.de
Translation: Marie Frohling, Fairfax/USA
Map (p. 96f.): Matthias Frach, Berlin
Cover design: Bauer+Möhring, Berlin, with photographs by Günter Schneider
Typesetting and page layout: Prill Partners | producing, Barcelona
Lithography: Bild1Druck GmbH, Berlin
Printing and binding: Westermann Druck Zwickau GmbH, Zwickau

ISBN 978-3-89773-942-0

ELBE

NEUSTADT

Bremer Str.

Hamburger Str.

Magdeburger Str.

Schäferstr.

Schweriner Str.

Fröbelstr.

Freiberger Str.

Ammonstr.

ALTSTADT

Leipziger Str.

Antonstr.

Könneritzstr.

Hansastr.

Bautzner Str.

Albertstr.

Glacisstr.

Rothenbgr. Görlitzer Str.

Terrassenufer

Pillnitzer St

Petersburger Str.

Bürgerwiese

Lennéstraße

Zoo

Tie

Zellescher Weg